My Cat, Nip

Written by Omar Ali

Illustrated by Lee Kwan

Decodable Book 6

Word Family -an	**Word Family -at**
can	cat
	mat

Word Family -in	**Word Family -ip**
bin	Nip
in	tip

High-Frequency Words

for	my	she
look	see	the
me		

I look for my cat.

Nip?

I tip the bin.

Nip looks in a cab.

She looks in a can.

She can see me.

I see my cat!

Nip!

Nip can nap on a mat.